The Bipolar Disorder Manual

ISBN 0-9758980-1-9

© 2004

By Shay Villere

Table of Contents

Foreword 3

Initial Feelings 4

Being In The Hospital 6

Getting Out Of The Hospital 8

Going To Therapy 9

Taking Medication 10

Working With Your Support System 11

Having Fun 12

Getting Back To Work/School 13

Progressing With Life 15

Relapses 16

Sleep 17

How To Explain What It Is Like To Be Bipolar 18

Helping Others 19

The Miracle Of Faith 20

The Bipolar Manual (Hospital Edition) 21

Foreword

So, you've just been diagnosed with bipolar disorder, also known as manic depression. The first thing I want to tell you is that the world is not over! Life does continue. Even though you are probably looking through this booklet while in a psychiatrist's office or a hospital room, life does go on - and happily, I might add! The fact that you have this disorder is simply another challenge to deal with, and should be regarded as such. Of course, being bipolar is a special challenge. It's not like studying for a test or performing well in a sporting event. It comes with a whole new group of emotions and situations. What this booklet will do is help you get through the next few months of your life. Even though you may only read these pages once, feel free to refer back to certain passages or to earmark pages that you find especially helpful. You may need them again in the future.

Initial Feelings

Well, here you are! You've got a mental disorder. It's an illness that affects your emotions, your thoughts, your mood, and your life in general. You will now be dealing with medications, therapy, and regular visits to the doctor's office. Is it a big problem? Yes. Can it be turned into a little problem? Yes. Will it destroy your life? Absolutely not, and here's why:

You are angry. You don't know why you have to deal with what you're going through. You're probably upset about the whole experience and you feel like you'd rather just rewind to a few months ago before you discovered that you are a little different than the mainstream population. You may have missed a little school or work time because of a hospital visit that probably lasted a week or two. Now you need to know how to deal with the overwhelming emotions going through your mind. Well, here's the good news - today there are a number of solutions for patients with bipolar disorder. There are a large group of therapies, medications, and job opportunities that are available to folks who need them. So stop being angry! Help is definitely available.

You are probably feeling relatively helpless. Lately the thoughts that have been going through your mind have been some of the worst things you've ever imagined. You've been suicidal, angry, sad, and exuberant - all in the span of a few minutes! They have been an incredibly tough combination of emotions and you're wondering how you're going to deal with all of them for the remainder of your life. Plus, you're probably losing a lot of sleep and you're wondering if you'll ever be able to relax again. Well, I have some good news for you. There are many of us that have done it! I can't lie to you. We lose some folks. In extreme circumstances where the stress gets too high and the medical and social support isn't strong enough, some patients die. But I'm one of the survivors, and I can show you how to be one too.

Take all of the feelings that have been flying through that noggin of yours...and share them! Tell everybody about them. Tell your doctors, your friends, and your family. Let everybody know what's going on. The #1 rule to being bipolar is NOT KEEPING THINGS IN! Let everything out. And don't spare a single feeling. Let everybody know everything. Even if you're a secretive person, learn to share. Sharing your feelings is the most important lesson to successfully living with bipolar disorder. You will be using this technique for your entire life, so you might as well practice it now.

Relax! Don't do stressful activities. Put everything on hold. Let go of the world for the next week or two. Give yourself some time to come down from everything you've just been through. Being in the hospital or going through several doctor's visits is extremely hard for ANYBODY. Don't bother stressing yourself out with extra duties. Take a break and get back to work after you have recovered.

Have some fun! Don't take this to mean go out and get liquored up. At this point in your life the one thing you don't need is drugs and/or alcohol. Not only can they interfere with your medications, but also folks with bipolar disorder can experience a TRUE loss of control when they are high/drunk. When I say, "Have fun!" I mean that you should do things you like to do. Whether it's fishing, playing ball, traveling, whatever.... just do it! Like Nike says. Go out and have some fun! With the new adjustments in your life, you're going to have to offset them with an additional amount of recreation. Odds are that some of your medications will create some unpleasant side effects. The more time you spend doing things you enjoy, the less brainpower you'll waste focusing on your new situation.

Being In The Hospital

You either already have been, or eventually will be, in the hospital. Even if it is only for a day or so to sleep off a bad episode, bipolar folks tend to spend some time in the hospital. The biggest thing to remember is that it's not a big deal! Being in the hospital can even be fun. It is boring every now and then, but being able to talk to the other patients, getting their perspective on life and mental illness, can be extremely enlightening. While you're in the hospital the best thing to do is make friends, sleep as much as you need to, and participate in as much therapy as possible. Remember not to be violent, listen to the facilitators, and let your doctor in on everything that's going through your mind.

The ability to deal with your doctor is a skill that is acquired over time. After being in the hospital five times and dealing with several doctors, I've realized that there is one key ingredient to establishing a wonderful relationship with him/her – the truth! Speak nothing but the truth to your doctor. Let him know absolutely everything. He's there to help, he's there to help you avoid having to come back, and he's there to improve your life in the long run. Lying to your doctor is a big mistake, mainly because it will probably result in him/her setting you up with the wrong medication and therapy regimen. Trust me…what you want more than anything is to get treated properly. Walking out of the hospital with the wrong treatment program is a TERRIBLE thing. This is a road you definitely don't want to go down, so tell the truth.

Make friends! There's nothing that the hospital staff wants more than seeing you getting along with all of the other patients. Not only does this improve your image to the people who are in control, but also it's fun! Being able to talk to everyone and have conversations about your lives is a very important component to enjoying your time in the hospital. Patients not only want to open up, but you can LEARN from them! Most of the patients will probably be older than you, so they will usually have some decent insight into mental illness. Plus, it will give you an opportunity to TALK ABOUT YOUR OWN PROBLEMS!!! And there is nothing better while you're in the hospital than talking about your problems. You will only get 15 or so minutes with your doctor each day, so talking to others will give you more opportunities to get things off your chest. There will be other therapies each day, but one-on-one with another person is always helpful.

SLEEP!!!! If you need to lie down, do it! Take a nap! Take two naps! Guess what? You're in the hospital. It doesn't matter! That's what they want you to do, anyway. They want you to rest and get better. And sleep often does that for bipolar patients. Often times you need opportunities to physically adjust to new medications or to just recover from a really bad episode. And the beds are usually pretty comfortable. So, if you need some rest, take it.

Do the therapy! Every single opportunity you get to participate in a therapeutic session, TAKE IT! Participation is part of the success formula for getting out of the hospital as soon as possible. The facilitators and your doctor keep track of all the times you go to therapy and participate in that therapy, so the more you go, the better. Plus, the therapy is usually quite fun. Remember that the key to getting out of the hospital is GETTING BETTER!! Therapy is a main component to getting better. I noticed during my first couple of trips to the hospital that there were numerous patients who "refused" to participate in the therapy. Well, a few days later they weren't refusing, mainly because they were watching patient after patient leave the hospital and go home because of the progress they had made in therapy. So don't waste any time and go to as much therapy as they offer.

Getting Out Of The Hospital

There are two simple things you need to remember when it comes to successfully being released from the hospital. The first is telling the truth. Each and every time you have a therapy session or meet with your psychiatrist, you have the option of telling the truth or not. Many patients believe that the best thing to do is cover up their problem. So they go into therapy meetings and lie, and then they go into their doctor and lie. Their assumption is that by lying about their feelings, making themselves appear healthier than they are, they will improve their chances of getting released. Now, while there is some sense in that, it is still not the best thing to do because it hurts your LONG TERM RECOVERY chances. The fact is that if you aren't feeling well, TELL THEM! If you're not better yet, TELL THEM. Don't put yourself in the position of ending up back in the hospital two weeks later because you lied about your mental stability. Trust me, it's not fun. Been there done that. Its much better to focus on making your first trip to the hospital your last one.

The second bit of advice that will help you get out of the hospital is STAYING OUT OF THE QUIET ROOM! The Quiet Room, as you might already know, is a room with a bed – with restraints. That is where they put patients who are disorderly. Coming from a man who has spent more than a few nights in the Quiet Room, it is definitely best to avoid it altogether. Don't cause trouble. Don't get into arguments with other patients, and DON'T BE VIOLENT. Some patients have trouble getting this into their heads, either because they are too busy trying to kill themselves or because they don't understand that the more time they spend in the Quiet Room, the longer they'll be in the hospital altogether.

Be patient, be passive, learn what you can, take your meds, and you'll be out of the hospital in no time.

Going To Therapy

"Oh Wizened Bipolar Veteran…knower of all ways to deal with the disorder that disorders us, what do we do after we've gotten out of the hospital?"

"Don't fret, child, for this world's mental experts have it all worked out. And the first thing on the agenda is to start in with some regularly scheduled therapy!"

Yep! The movies and the books don't lie. Therapy fixes lots of things, and it definitely can take the edge off of being Bipolar. Odds are that after you get out of the hospital you will be required to go to a daily/weekly group therapy session for a couple of weeks. These sessions are not only therapeutic, but they are also extremely fun, believe it or not. You see, when you go around every day existing amongst other people that DON'T have Bipolar Disorder, it is EXTREMELY comforting to spend an hour or so a day with some folks that DO know how you feel and DO know what you're talking about. Granted, they won't all be your age, and they probably won't be people you'd really want to hang out with on a regular basis, but the INSIGHT that some of these folks have will just clean knock your socks off. A good portion of the folks in the room will tell you that they've been dealing with this illness for years. Their help, as well as the social worker or psychologist assigned to facilitate the group, will truly make a difference in your life. So don't blow off your therapy appointments! They are important! And they can definitely keep you from having a…dare I say it? RELAPSE.

Taking Medication

"But I'm feeling much better now! I'm not depressed. I'm not hyper. I can go to work. I can take care of my daily responsibilities. Why should I have to take regular medication?"

Oh, my young naïve bipolar outpatient, you are new to the ways of this disease. The reason you take the medication is to avoid a relapse, and I'll tell you why.
With bipolar disorder, everything can be going absolutely peachy. Life can seem like one big box of chocolate. Then, in comes the dreaded beast…STRESS! Something can happen in your life, like a relative dying or losing your job, or possibly marital stress. Then the walls come crashing down. All of the work you have put into managing your emotions and watching your behavior don't mean a hill of beans because now you're flying again. Your emotions are going up and down like Space Mountain and its only a matter of a couple sleepless days and then you find yourself in the hospital again, even if its been many years since your last visit.

However, guess what? There are a number of wonderful medications that can keep that sort of thing from happening, as well as help you enjoy life a little more. These medications have TRULY changed my life and allowed me to do a host of things that I never thought possible right after I was diagnosed. I take a few pills in the morning, a few pills in the evening, and even when life gets EXTRA hairy, I still don't get so out of wack that I have to go to the hospital. And trust me, if I never have to go to the hospital for the rest of my life….that is fine by me!

So take your meds. They help. And if you feel like your meds aren't working for you, talk to your psychiatrist. In today's world there are many different options and if one med isn't working for you, another can.

Working With Your Support System

Who's your support system? Your friends, your family, your doctor, your pets, your priest, your rabbi, your kids, your bed, your bathtub, your books, your computer....ANYTHING AND EVERYTHING that makes you feel good about yourself! When you're bipolar, you may need help at any given time. You never know when something will kick in and an episode might occur. So utilize anybody and anything that might be able to calm you down and help you get stable again.

Over the years I've run the whole spectrum. I've been to my psychiatrist, I've had late night talks with my parents, I've spent four hours in a bathtub, I've hugged my dog, I've slept 12 hours a day...WHATEVER WAS NEEDED to feel balanced again. Remember that there are two main goals for the average bipolar patient: don't commit suicide and don't get in a position where hospitalization is necessary. Now, you might laugh at that statement. You might be someone who has only been in the hospital once, or maybe never, and you don't think something like that will happen. Well, I'm sorry to burst your bubble. There will probably be times in the future where you will think back on those two goals and realize why I mentioned them.

For me, whenever I get really stressed or worried, or when I lose sleep...I start thinking about suicide. It is not fun, and I don't consciously choose to do it, but the thoughts are there. So, a long time ago I set up a PRIME DIRECTIVE for myself – no suicide! No matter what happened, no matter how bad things got, even if I had to spend months in a hospital – I still wasn't going to kill myself. You need to make it a goal for yourself, too. Bipolar disorder is a nasty illness, and the 20% death rate doesn't come from heart attacks.

So, use what you've got! If you feel like you don't have enough of a support system, create one! Make more friends! Get a hot tub! Get some pets! Get a girlfriend or a boyfriend!

Having Fun

Having fun sounds easy, huh? Well, its not, not if you're in the middle of a bad depression. You may already know what I'm talking about. Nothing sounds interesting, people that usually make you laugh are making you cry, your sleep schedule is either nonexistent or completely switched around, and working is next to impossible. So, you know what you have to do to take care of all that? WORK at HAVING FUN.

I know it sounds kind of silly. The idea of actually putting effort into having fun does sound silly, but you have to do it. You have to deliberately inject enjoyable activities into your normal routine in order to keep that big bogeyman called depression out of your life. Get used to it because this is going to be necessary for the rest of your physical life. Don't let a single day go by without some fun. Whether it be watching one of your favorite movies, calling a friend, or taking a three week trip to Australia to scuba dive, DO IT! This is actually one of the most important lessons in this entire manual, so clue in while you can. There will come a time when you will go a few days without some real in-your-face fun and then you'll remember what you read here and immediately go out and enjoy yourself in order to alleviate whatever problem is circulating in your mind.

Schedule fun regularly! Trust me, you'll need it.

Getting Back To Work/School

Oh boy, now this is a toughie. If you are a student you will find this especially challenging. I say this because fellow employees and bosses are more inclined to appreciate what you're dealing with than fellow high school students. In my junior year of high school I returned from a two-week stay in the hospital and discovered that life had truly changed. Everybody looked at me differently, my friends acted differently, and dealing with everything became quite challenging. I was still at a point where my medications weren't working correctly, and at that point in my life it was taking so much energy just to handle my own mind that to ask me to deal with constant undue pressure at school was too much. I battled with this issue for months, packing an additional two-week hospital stay in between four more months of school. Eventually, it got to be too much, and I took the equivalency exam. But next fall I entered college and now I have a bachelor of science in Management Information Systems, and I'm working on my MBA. My story aside, the advice I'm going to give in regards to this situation is pretty basic and that is Realize There Is An Alternative.

In life there is ALWAYS another option. Even if you can't comprehend it at this very moment, there is ALWAYS another path to take. If you can no longer deal with the situation at your school or your job, you can always negotiate another situation. And, as with everything in human life, you can always start over. If school problems get too deep, you can always change schools. If job problems get too stressful you can change jobs. Understand that no matter how tough things are in your current situation you can always switch things around. While I was trying to figure things out in high school, my principal allowed me to switch my schedule around. He also gave me special privileges in order to better facilitate my own healing.

At one of my jobs, things just got to be too much and I started crying in front of one of my supervisors. A six foot seven inch computer technician started weeping, all because of a bad situation with my then girlfriend. But it didn't matter. My boss understood that sometimes adults have problems that overwhelm them. He wasn't even bothered by it. He told me to do whatever I had to do to feel better and that if I needed time off I could have it. The fact of the matter was that I was a valued employee and if I had a little problem that required some attention, it didn't bother him. Employers constantly deal with this kind of stuff. Its normal! Do not worry about it. You know what? If your boss goes crazy when you need to deal with some personal issues, you probably shouldn't be working there anyway. The day of the super anal boss is gone. In a working environment the atmosphere is much more tailored to keeping valuable employees happy. Happier employees means more efficiency, and that's what the game of business is all about. So don't stress!

Remember, the people in charge are usually willing to help. And if they're not, this world always has another path to walk down. Don't worry if you need to take one.

Progressing With Life

Oh, the joy of life. Sometimes fun, sometimes not, but always progressing. Whether you like it or not, you're always moving along. Until the Lord calls you home, you've got to keep on going. And absolutely the best advice to give to a bipolar patient about progressing with life is this – let go.

That's it. Let go! Let go of your problems, let go of your preconceived notions about life…let go of stress. Learn to drop things at the tip of a hat. Learn to drop fights and learn to makeup. Learn to drop your pride, drop your ego, and drop everything you thought you knew. Unfortunately, or maybe fortunately, once you're bipolar you don't have time to get caught up in unnecessary junk. You've got to learn to ebb and flow and fly and run, all without petty junk creeping up on you. So let go, give in to Love, and let the fear slide off of you. It's a great world, but you've got to open your eyes to it. It's a little tougher when you're bipolar, but trust me, it CAN be done.

Relapses

Oh the joyous world of relapses! I know quite a bit about these because I had five hospitalizations in the first six years after I was diagnosed. Each time I thought I was never going back. However, at the moment it has been almost four years since I was hospitalized, and hopefully I won't be back for a while. When you're Bipolar I such as I am, there's always the possibility. Major stress tends to beat you up quite a bit, and bad timing can always create another few days sleeping off some unfortunate life circumstances. So be ready for them!

Remember that relapses aren't a big deal. They happen. You can do your best, take all your meds, go to therapy, but you may still have to be hospitalized. So don't beat yourself up if that happens. There's no point in putting any extra worry into the situation. If you have to go you have to go. The important thing to remember is that it is better to be in the hospital if you need it than out of the hospital causing extra damage to your life. Also, an experienced bipolar patient can bring in the reins on himself/herself pretty quickly. So if you need to get some help, it will usually only result in three or four days of attention.

Also….keep up your medical insurance! I can't stress this enough. When you're bipolar you have GOT to have medical insurance ALL the time. You need it to pay for your meds, you need it to cover hospital costs, and you need it to get therapy when necessary. NEVER let your medical insurance slide. There are many folks in some bad, BAD situations because they couldn't afford help when they needed it.

Sleep

I cannot even begin to tell you how important sleep is to a bipolar patient. The amount of sleep you get will make or break your life. Go to bed too late, get up too early, and suddenly the next day is SO MUCH harder than it normally would be. This is true for lots of people, even those who are not bipolar, but for those of us with the illness the effect is tremendously magnified.

Feelings kind of rule your world when you're bipolar. When your feelings are positive, life is a bowl of cherries, but when you feel tired, stressed out, or anxious…man, life sure does get hard! So, make sure that to avoid undue problems – get your sleep. I'm not exaggerating when I say that it can mean the difference between life and death. The suicidal thoughts pop up with much more frequency and with higher intensity when sleep is escaping you. So if you're tired during the day, take a nap. If you have things to do early in the morning, go to bed when you should. Go through life as happy as possible. Get enough sleep!

How To Explain What It Is Like To Be Bipolar

So, you have friends, you have family, and none of them really know what bipolar disorder is. That's okay. When you explain it to them, keep it simple. Tell them that it means your emotions are intensified and that your highs are higher than most people's but your lows are also much lower than most people's. There's nothing wrong with telling them that you're on medication. Heck, all of us have to take medication at some point in our lives. And feel free to explain to them that you have gone to some therapy. In this new century, therapy is now a typical thing. Lots of people do it. Nobody is really going to judge you for it.

Make sure to keep things in a positive light. Don't go into the really horrible side of this illness unless you truly feel like enlightening someone. Most people don't need to know that suicidal thoughts are typical and that if things get too stressful you could pop. Just give them the basic facts and if they really want to research more you can send them to the informational webpage of your choice. Or, I guess you could give them this booklet.

Helping Others

Along with everything else you're doing to help yourself, start by doing some volunteer work. I don't necessarily mean structured volunteer work where you go somewhere for a certain number of hours and do work you don't like. I mean other stuff like spending time with your kids, helping out your parents, being a good friend and spouse. Be generous with yourself. For bipolar people it is especially important to share yourself. We don't necessarily get along too well if we're not constantly opening ourselves up to other parts and people of the world. You'll find that opportunities will come along each and every day to show someone else you are a spectacular person. Don't pass them up!

The Miracle of Faith

Now, I've given you the lowdown on just about every important part of being bipolar: the hard stuff to handle, the easy stuff, the positives and the negatives. Now I'm going to give you a little tip that has truly helped me – believing in God. Those of you that are agnostic or atheist may balk at this sort of thing, but let me fill you in on something. When you are at your worst, when you are in bed fighting off a bad episode, you are going to need a light at the end of the tunnel. Without that light, without that love, the world could easily crater in on top of you. Believing in God has saved lots of people from ending their life prematurely, and it can do the same for you. If you're skeptical about this, then I suggest you try it and if it doesn't work for you then give it up. But trying it should be first on your list. I should know – without my belief in God you wouldn't be reading this.

The Bipolar Disorder Manual

HOSPITAL EDITION

ISBN 0-9758980-5-1

© 2004

By Shay Villere

Table of Contents (Hospital Edition)

Foreword	23
Your Episode	25
Emergency Room	27
Getting Evaluated	30
Ambulance Ride	32
Quiet Room	33
Roommates	35
Meeting Time	36
Leisure Time	38
Sessions With Your Psychiatrist	40
Attending Counselors	42
Field Trips	44
Game Time	46
Visitor Time	47
Making Friends	48
Your Meds	50
Getting Discharged	52
The End	53
Appendix: Topics to Remember	54
About The Author	56

Foreword

It has been about two years since I wrote "The Bipolar Disorder Manual". It was written completely on a whim, with no future plans to sell or distribute it. I was unemployed for a few months after graduating from college, and my parents suggested that I take advantage of that time and do some writing. I wrangled with the idea for a while, already pretty busy with the website I'd been running for a few years, but I finally decided that "The Bipolar Disorder Manual" should be written. Even if no one else ever read it, I would still get satisfaction from the creative process.

Since I was unemployed, the writing portion only took about a month or so. I would write a new chapter every few days, and soon enough I had a nifty little book. I filed it away with all my other projects, and within a few months I had all but forgotten about it. Shoot to a year and a half later.

I'd gotten what I considered to be a dream job, working in the IT field under the management of one of my best friends. The company that employed us turned out to be possibly the best bank in America. I had married the woman of my dreams the previous year, and our house was already filled with three wonderful pets. Things were going so well that I could barely imagine what else there was to do in life. Then it struck me!

In the first few months that Kelly and I were married, I had sold a bunch of our excess belongings on eBay. The process had been quick and easy, and I marveled at the power of the website. It only took a few days to realize the opportunities that lay before me; I could sell my writing! Within a few months I had four books selling on eBay, "The Bipolar Disorder Manual" being the most successful. The eBay success led me to look into other distribution options, and at the present moment I can say that my books are flying around the Internet faster than I can track them. They are sold in some places, given away for free in others, and all I can do is marvel at the glorious ways in which God has blessed me!

For a while I thought "The Bipolar Disorder Manual" had covered everything. I felt that I had touched on every single topic that a new bipolar patient would be interested in. Then one day I was driving home from work, my mind wandering as usual, and it came to me. The most important topic in the manual needed more attention. It needed its own book. It was in that moment that "The Bipolar Disorder Manual – Hospital Edition" was born.

You'll find that the information you're about to take in is invaluable. You'll discover ways to deal with the people and events that make up a visit to a mental health facility. My five visits have given me insights to help guide you in the right direction. As you learned in the last book, my methods are proven – I've got everything a person could ask for: an amazing wife, plenty of friends, a dream job, and the most important thing of all, inner happiness!

Pay attention to what is in this book. Study it as carefully and dutifully as you can. Not only can it help you through your next hospital visit, but in certain circumstances it can save your life! This is not just another advice book. This is knowledge that comes from a first hand source, straight from a guy who has been through it. Don't be surprised if you've never heard about some of these methods, because unless you know someone like me, odds are that a group therapy session or psychiatrist's couch haven't supplied you with them. I know, because I've been there!

Enjoy your time with "The Bipolar Disorder Manual – Hospital Edition". Keep it handy. Send it to friends who might benefit from it. Most of all, don't hesitate to whip it out when you are wondering about something. I do know the path through it all, and aside from Jesus himself, I may be the best person to hear this from.

Good luck, and God bless!

Your Episode

Your episode was probably similar to my episode(s). For weeks, the people around you were able to tell that something was wrong with you, but you were completely unable to pick up on it yourself. Your ego probably inflated, you might have been delusional about who you were or what you could do, and you might have experienced some paranoia. This is all completely normal for a serious bipolar condition. People such as myself, who are Bipolar I, experience these symptoms to an extremely serious degree when we have an episode. Sometimes a hospital visit is the only thing that will snap us out of our trip down the rabbit hole. That's okay though, because the fact that there is help in the first place is a beautiful thing. For less fortunate people throughout history, there have not been any options. In this time, in this country, we are truly blessed!

Hopefully you were not violent during your episode. Violence changes the whole spectrum of your experience. If you were violent, it is possible that you were arrested. If you were arrested, then after you are released from the hospital you may be going to jail. How do I know this? I was violent during one of my episodes and I was subsequently arrested and tried for these acts after I was released from the hospital. I was lucky, though, because I never had to spend any time in jail thanks to a nice letter from my psychiatrist. With my parents support, the judge decided that I had learned my lesson and the charges were dropped. But jail can happen, and so do your best not to be violent. While TV and movies might have you believe that people get off the hook when they have a mental illness, this is not completely true, so watch it.

During your episode you were probably impaired due to lack of sleep. When a bipolar patient is revving up to their eventual break, they usually have been influenced by several nights of little to no sleep. The wonderful thing about going to the hospital is that this long string of sleepless nights will fall by the wayside. You'll finally be able to sleep as much as you would like. The staff will provide medication that will calm you down and enable you to relax the way you need to. This is yet another wonderful benefit of going to the hospital. You get the rest you need, so take advantage of the opportunity. Some people go through their whole lives without really being able to get proper rest.

The most important thing to remember about your episode is that it is indeed forgettable! You can walk away from episodes. You can get to a point in life where there is no need for them to happen. You can get the proper medication and therapy, and life can definitely return to normal. My last hospital visit was nine years ago, and during that time I have flourished! I've gotten a bachelor of science, I'm working on my MBA, I have a wonderful wife, and my career is progressing in an extremely positive fashion. All of this was possible because I was able to take advantage of my time in the hospital. I used it to get what I needed – the right medications, the right therapy, and the right downtime. I relaxed, I made friends, I contributed to other patients' progress, and I succeeded in getting out in a timely fashion. The amount of time you have to spend in the hospital depends completely on how you approach your stay. If you are positive about things, and cooperate, then you will probably be out in less than two weeks. If you take a different approach, then you could be looking at months.

I strongly suggest that you pay attention to the rest of the chapters in this book. The advice is valuable, the language is simple, and the knowledge you gain from it could help you for the rest of your life.

Emergency Room

Once upon a time, in another life, I decided to throw a swing at an emergency room attendant. This lead to the arrest described in the last chapter. I'm not proud of it. I try to forget about it. The next time I had an episode I actually apologized to him for it. Why did I throw that swing? Because one of the doctors asked me why I thought I needed to be there. My dad had brought me there in the middle of the night because I was feeling horribly manic. After four hours of observation with no symptoms they told me to go home, so I proceeded to give them some proof of my condition. My dad felt badly because he didn't act fast enough to jump between us. It all happened too fast. Please don't follow in my footsteps. I am including that story here so you understand how important it is to verbally get your message across to the emergency room staff without using force. They need to understand what is going on in order to treat you properly, so verbally help them as much as you can. At the emergency room the policy is pretty much observation. If you do not feel you are a danger to either yourself or to someone else, and you are not producing psychotic symptoms, then you might as well be at home. If you don't need emergency room attention, then you shouldn't be there. You can wait until regular office hours and call your regular doctor. On the other hand, if you're suicidal or a danger to someone else, the ER is heaven on Earth. There's no better place to be. A psychiatrist will evaluate you, you'll get the proper medication, and if necessary you'll be hospitalized. I highly recommend an emergency room trip if you feel like you need it.

Your average trip to the emergency room could last three hours or more, so get ready to wait. You will not be rushed in and rushed out. They may set you up in a separate room to wait, but you'll basically just need to be patient. Don't make problems, don't be violent, just wait your turn.

During one of my trips I was under the impression that I was a key member of the Second Coming of Christ. When a clock struck eight o'clock in the morning, I went berserk and started screaming. I fell on the floor in self-induced convulsions, positive that I was contributing to God's Master Plan. Was I right? Probably not, because a few seconds later I was strapped to a gurney headed to the hospital. A few years of experience have shown me that several mental patients experience the exact same thing when under the influence of a severe manic episode. My advice to you if you find yourself in the same situation is this: tell somebody! Let somebody know what's going on. The best thing you can do for yourself is to let someone in on the madness flowing through your mind. Not only will you receive help faster, but you'll feel a whole lot better after you unload those thoughts.

Sometimes during emergency room trips, neophyte bipolar patients get scared, and don't really want to tell the evaluating psychiatrist what's wrong. This is the worst thing you can possibly do. That is what they are there for, after all! They are there to help you! They are there to listen and get you the help you need. Keep in mind that doesn't always mean a trip the hospital. Sometimes they will just set up a doctor's appointment for the next morning. Emergency room visits don't always end in the Quiet Room, which we'll talk about later. So remember that when you make the trip to the ER, you are taking care of yourself. You are making sure nothing crazy happens while your disorder is doing a number on you.

A lot of new patients have no idea what it is like to really go full force into a manic or suicidal episode. Well, let me tell you that it is not fun. A lot of folks don't even make it out of them alive. Speaking as one who has, I want to convey to you how important it is to have a cutoff switch. You must work really hard at training your mind to just pull the switch if need be.

You must be able to sit or lie down, and allow others to care for you. I call it the "Prime Directive". You must be able to say to yourself, "I will not die today. I absolutely positively will take every step necessary to stay alive." This is a must. I suspect most successful bipolar patients have one of these. We are able to just stop the actions, and just lie down. Without this ability you are in trouble. If you don't master this, there will come a time when people will have to bring you down. You may have to spend time in jail, or you may be severely drugged for long periods of time. Take my advice and develop a Prime Directive. It could save your life some time, or like it did for me, many times.

Getting Evaluated

During the end of your trip to the Emergency Room, you'll receive a visit. Not Santa Claus, not the Easter Bunny, but someone who holds the key to where you will spend your next two weeks to two months – a psychiatrist.

In most major cities across the United States, for every hospital, there is a team of psychiatrists that is on call for cases such as yours. It may take them two or three hours to get to you, but be thankful they are there. Do not think they are taking their own sweet time in getting to you. They are usually in another part of the city seeing someone in another emergency room. Remember that on any given night, there can be quite a few people who come to emergency rooms with mental health issues. Your case does matter to them, though, and they will get to you. When your visitor does come it may be just one person, or it may be more than one.

When he or she shows up, tell the truth. Don't hold anything back. The professional needs to know everything that is circulating inside your brain. A lot of folks are tempted to lie, but it doesn't do any good because it is not just what you say that lets them know you are sick. You may not realize it, but when you're really screwed up there are a million outward signs, and the psychiatrist can pick up on all of them. It really helps the situation if you just come out with everything. It means that your medication and therapy needs will be more quickly and more accurately determined.

The psychiatry team members are usually really nice. A lot of folks see them as "members of the establishment", or as "people who judge you", but that's not true at all. They are important members of an important team, the team that is going to try and get you healthy again. So take them seriously, answer their questions truthfully, and do your best to stay in their good graces. After all, your goal is a speedy hospital stay, or better yet, no hospital stay at all, right? I'm fully convinced that the first time I went to the hospital fifteen years ago I literally bought myself an extra few days by being kind of a jerk in the beginning. This was the first and last time I took that route. So be nice, cooperate, and you'll get through this thing. It's a piece of cake, as I'll show you throughout this book.

Ambulance Ride

Ah, the joy of an ambulance ride! Two guys show up, cart you off, and the whole time you're wondering, "What did I do to deserve this?"

During one of my ambulance rides I was fully convinced that I was already dead and this was one of the ways people were delivered to heaven, via the heavenly ambulance. You can imagine the crazy stuff that was coming out of my mouth. I was talking to the attendants like they were angels. I explained to them how I was so happy to be going to heaven. I was fully gone, essentially. But it's okay, because these guys do this all the time and they're used to it. So don't worry about what you say, just relax and don't fight anything. They've got everything under control.

In my opinion the best thing to do during the ride is to sleep. You've got twenty or thirty minutes on a nice comfy cot, so just relax and let the Z's begin. At the moment all you have to do is kick back and be happy that you're somewhere safe. Your mind has been putting you through a lot lately, so now's the time for the relaxation to begin.

Once again, the main tip here is to relax. Don't fight these guys and don't be aggressive. Just be kind, chill out, and let them do their job. They're in it to help you, just like everyone else during your hospital stay. You'll be okay as long as you realize that. Too many patients want to fight it every step of the way, but my method is much more successful.

Relax, relax, relax! You will be back in the swing of it in no time, but for now, its healing time. Use it wisely.

Quiet Room

While you are in the hospital, you have one goal that is more important than all the others – you MUST stay out of the Quiet Room!

The Quiet Room is the classic rubber-walled room that you have seen numerous times on TV and in the movies, with one difference: there is no padding on the walls. "Why not?" you ask. Well, you probably won't be touching the walls or the floor. Instead you'll probably be strapped to the bed for your own protection.

Yes, there are leather restraints in Quiet Rooms and they are used. If you are seriously out of control, you'll find yourself in them. Don't think that the attendants won't leave you in there, because they will if your behavior warrants it.. If you can't get it together, then you'll stay in there. If you don't respond, you will stay restrained. And trust me, it is not fun at all!

The medical staff will be doing their best to juggle your meds properly, so while you're in the Quiet Room take your meds the way they ask you to. Granted, these meds may make you really sleepy, and you may wonder where the last few hours have gone, but that's okay. Like I've said before, you're in the hospital to rest.

There are all kinds of ways you can be restrained in the Quiet Room. They can completely restrain you, or they can have you on your stomach or your back. Or, they can just restrain your feet, or there can be no restraints at all. In fact, they may even leave the door open and ask you not to leave, all to see if you can obey their orders. So listen to them, do what they ask, and you'll be spared unnecessary time in there.

Remember, like everything else in the hospital, this room is there to help you. It is meant to keep you safe when you may be a menace to yourself and/or other people. So take my advice and don't rebel against it. It will only cause you more stress and buy you a few extra days or weeks in the hospital.

Roommates

The great thing about your roommate situation is that the powers that be have taken care to match patients accordingly. They are not going to put you in a room with someone with whom you will mix badly. At least they will try not to!

During my five visits I roomed with a number of people. Usually folks only stay in the hospital for a couple weeks, therefore there is frequent switching. This is usually not a hassle, because you will probably only have a few belongings in your room anyway. If you are asked to switch rooms, just gather your stuff in your arms and walk to where you are told.

One of my roommates was considerably older than me by about fifty years. This created a little bit of a problem because he constantly had medical personnel coming in to check on him, sometimes while I was sleeping. He was a kind gentleman though, so it didn't bother me a whole lot. Be prepared for this, because sometimes a mental hospital is just a stop-off for someone that is on their way to another type of medical facility.

Something you need to keep in mind is that often you will be in a room with someone who is suicidal. Now, these people usually have an attendant with them 24-7, but sometimes someone slips through the cracks. If you are ever on the receiving end of a "suicide plan confession", the first thing you should do is tell an attendant. Trust me, you don't want someone to make an attempt when you could've done something about it. While you are in the hospital, you will probably see some patients with bandages wrapped around their wrists. Those bandages didn't get there by accident. Unstable patients can do some pretty crazy things sometimes.

In general, you will probably not have to worry about your roommate. You will go about your business, he/she will go about theirs, and you'll both be out of the hospital without incident.

Meeting Time

In mental health facilities there is usually a morning meeting where all the patients, their attendants, and possibly some other staff meet to discuss everyone's progress. As with just about every other aspect of life, the hospital expects you to perform as a patient. You set personal goals, you do follow-ups, and your behavior is critiqued just as if you were an employee at a job. If you do not meet the expectations that have been set, the negative consequences are quite simple – your stay lasts longer.

During my five hospitalizations, I have seen patients treat meeting time and their personal goals in very different ways. Some patients took the meetings seriously which helped them get discharged in a few days while others had to wait. That resistant behavior probably contributed to their lengthy stays. Now, if you are an adult, and all of the expense that goes into a hospitalization is on YOUR shoulders, make that an incentive to get discharged as soon as possible. If you are a kid, odds are that you will not be the one picking up the check. But it is always good to keep in mind that each hospital day runs about $2,000 to $3,000 dollars. Now, God-willing, you have insurance of some sort and you won't be paying all of this yourself, but it is still a good incentive to take things seriously. Besides, policies have limits on how may hospitalization days a person can have in a twelve month period. It makes sense to use them wisely!

During meeting time make sure to pay attention, take things seriously, and also be supportive of other patients. If you typically have trouble respecting other people, now is the time to work on that skill. Everybody is equal in the hospital and should get treated like the important human beings that they are. So, don't disparage anyone and don't get in any fights.

Remember, the less conflict the better. There will always be some patients who act out, but make sure you are not one of them!

Remind yourself constantly that you are being observed during your entire stay. In the meetings you will be given feedback on those observations, and you will have a chance to give your opinions too. Make sure you always tell the truth, and don't get angry if some criticism doesn't please you. These attendants, doctors, and nurses, are doing their best to get you healthy enough to be discharged. Don't slow your own progress by being impolite or haughty. Your hospital stay is a two-way street, and you don't want to create any red lights that don't need to be there.

You will be given a set of levels to work with. This means that depending on your performance you will move up and down the ladder. The goal is to reach the top level – being discharged! Some people move faster than others, so don't get discouraged if others seem to be progressing faster than you. A typical stay is probably at least a week, but it could be less and it could be more. Some patients manage to do it in a few days, but these folks usually fall into a different category of patient. Perhaps they have been to the hospital a few times before and know how to fast track their progress. I have been one of those patients. Of course, I've also been the patient who bangs his head on the door of the Quiet Room. You live, learn, and use your experience to your advantage, just like every other part of life. The hospital is no different.

If you use the Golden Rule in the meetings, which means that you treat everyone else the way you would like to be treated, you'll be fine. Keep in mind that no one is in there without reason. Everybody has their problems and is doing their best to deal with them. Don't extend your stay by mouthing off unnecessarily or giving attendants issues to use against you. They are interested in seeing you leave, but they do not want to discharge you until you are ready.

Leisure Time

If you have ever seen the movie "One Flew Over The Cuckoo's Nest", and been amazed at the amount of time that the patients spent just milling around, then I have some news for you – that is not far from the truth.

Yes, there are activities. Yes, there is therapy. Yes, you spend time speaking with your psychiatrist, and you spend time eating. HOWEVER, there is still a lot of time that is not predetermined for any given activity. There is at least an hour or two like this in the beginning of the day, and there is an hour or two like this at the end of the day. This is partly because patients often need lots of time for naps, and partly because you are in the hospital to relax! So they are just providing the time during which you can fulfill those aspects of your recovery.

Take advantage of these opportunities! Make friends! Play games! Be happy! These actions will all help to produce what you are really looking for in the first place – a quick trip home! The predispositions you project during your leisure time have a big effect on the length of your stay. If you spend time brooding by yourself, or smoking constantly, then you won't be getting out as fast as patients that participate in positive activities! Believe it or not, leisure time is extremely important. It is observed, as is everything else that you do. So don't let it go to waste!!!

Of course, leisure time can also mean naptime. There is nothing wrong with taking a nap once a day if you need it. The meds you'll be on will probably sap a decent amount of your energy, so don't stay up if you really need to hit the sheets for a little bit.

Here's a small tip that you may also want to keep in mind – don't spend every minute of your leisure time watching TV. While I don't have hard data supporting this conclusion, I'm of the opinion that too much TV watching could be looked upon in a bad light by the powers that be. If you fill your three to four hours of leisure time with nothing but soap operas and talk shows, you're probably not as well off as the guys who are taking walks around the yard and visiting with other patients and staff. As in most aspects of life, it pays to make friends, so you are better off doing that than becoming a couch potato.

Sessions With Your Psychiatrist

I will preface this chapter by saying something extremely pertinent to the discussion. During my hospital visits my psychiatrists were attentive, caring, enjoyable to work with, and very in tune with my needs. Not all of them are like this, so here is some advice to help you in either situation.

The psychiatrist during my first two hospitalizations was a very experienced doctor who actually turned out to be the father of a childhood friend. He was able to quickly and accurately diagnose my condition, which helped shorten my stay. My visits with him were usually short and sweet. I made sure to be upfront about what was going on in my mind. Also, in 1993 the medication list for bipolar disorder was not all that expansive, so the medication choices for me were few. Also, as one of my doctors told my mother, determining which medications to use can be as much an art as a science. He said that each person is unique. Their reactions to the same drug can never be predicted. My first bipolar medication was Lithium, and I was on it for four years.

The psychiatrist for my next two hospitalizations was another kind gentleman. These two stays lasted half as long as the ones two years previous, and that was probably because my condition was already diagnosed, but the medications still needed some tweaking. I learned something important during these visits. I learned that I could ask for privileges and, if at all possible, my psychiatrist was willing to grant them. For instance, I asked for a field trip with my parents and he gave it to me. I also asked to have an extended visiting time with my friends and he gave it to me. If I wanted to take a hot tub bath, he provided permission. My point in telling you all this is that you should not be afraid to ask your psychiatrist for things. Usually he will be the one who grants permission and there is no harm in asking. Even if he/she doesn't think it is a good idea right then, that doesn't mean it might not be okay in a day or so. So make sure you ask for anything you need or want.

When I was twenty-two, and my visit only lasted five days, my psychiatrist in the hospital was my psychiatrist in normal life. Which reminds me to tell you that my experience has been that while hospitalized a patient has a doctor other than one's regular doctor. These doctors are on the hospital's in-house staff and usually do not see patients outside the hospital. However, sometimes a doctor may do rotations, which means he/she will do both at different times. That is what happened to me when I was twenty-two. My personal psychiatrist happened to be on an in-house rotation the day I was admitted. So he knew exactly what I needed, my medication adjustments were fast and effective, and all I did was tell him the truth. The reason for this visit was that we had been experimenting with one of my dosages, and I made the mistake of letting one of them go too low. We both knew what the problem was, so during this visit we just put it back where it was before and that is where the dosage has been ever since.

Treat your psychiatrist like one of your friends, because that is what he is. He really is your best friend in the hospital. His judgment has the biggest effect on your wellness, so you need to make sure that if anybody in the entire place knows what's going on with you, it's him.

Another thing to remember is that your psychiatrist has several patients in the hospital, so his time is extremely limited. You may only be able to see him for a half hour or so each day. You've got to be happy with that, and don't fuss about it, because that will only buy you trouble. In the hospital you will constantly be seeing patients asking to see their psychiatrist, and the only thing this gets them is a negative notation on their record. Be patient! You will see him when you see him, and trust in his judgment. Remember, you do not know the medications better than he does!

Attending Counselors

You will come to know several people at the hospital quite intimately. These folks will be there when you are crying, they will be there when you can't sleep, and they'll be there to discuss your progress at the morning meetings. They are the attending counselors, and you'll need them more than you know.

When I first got admitted to the hospital back in 1992 at the tender age of sixteen, I was put on suicide watch. I hadn't attempted suicide, but that was the designation I was given due to the state of my mental health. When you're on suicide watch, you have a counselor with you twenty-four hours a day, seven days a week, no matter what you're doing. I thought this was a silly idea, until I ran into a couple nights where I couldn't sleep and I was relatively scared to be in a hospital for the first time. The counselor was there to talk me through it and provide the support that I needed.

You won't have the same attending counselor all the time. It's a job like any other and they have to go home at some point. But if you're in a good hospital, all the counselors will be extremely helpful and even though you'll have some favorites, everybody will take good care of you.

One of the number one things to remember with counselors is that they are people too. Several of the patients I spent time with treated the counselors like servants. I always found this practice to be ridiculous. If those patients ever knew how many extra hospitalization days they were probably buying themselves, I doubt they would have acted like that.

My advice is to treat the counselors like friends. They are there to hear your problems and they want to help you so make it easy on them! Not only will you get out of the hospital faster, but you will enjoy your stay more because you will get a reputation as a well behaved patient. Just be kind, polite, and you will be on your way home in no time.

Field Trips

During one of my hospital stays, we were offered a deal. If we progressed well for the next few days, and exhibited excellent behavior, we would be able to participate in a field trip. You are probably laughing at this, but it's true! One of the incentives that hospitals offer is field trips. They can be with family chaperones or with attending counselors. They can be for a few hours, or possibly even overnight. The one that I was a part of was a trip to an ice skating rink.

The funny part about my experience was that practically no one had the ability to ice skate. Sure, a few of us gave it a shot, but mostly it was an excuse to eat hot dogs and play video games. Granted, the goal of the trip was to get us some fresh air, some away time from the inside of the institution. But if you ask me, I would have appreciated a movie or a trip to the mall a whole lot more.

Now, don't expect these. I've been to the hospital five times, and I've only been offered this once. So, don't get angry if you never get this opportunity. The best thing to do is be on your best behavior, and if one of these chances rolls around then you can be included.

During one of my hospitalizations, a fellow patient was given a personal field trip. His father-in-law was being honored for an achievement of some sort, and the powers-that-be allowed his wife to pick him up, take him to the event, and then bring him back the next morning. I'm sure those of you who are inexperienced with the inner workings of a mental institution are questioning this practice, but let me assure you, these privileges are only given to patients who are very close to being released anyway. The patients who are still knocking around in the Quiet Room do not get these opportunities.

So, once again, notice how good behavior produces the reward. As I've already mentioned a few times: the better you behave, the sooner you'll get out. Life is all about producing the correct result at the correct time, and your stay in the hospital is no exception.

Game Time

The key thing to remember about game time is that it is an opportunity to get some physical activity. It is not really an opportunity to win, or dominate, or beat up on your opponent. The attendants don't want to see anyone be overly aggressive, or really even try that hard to win. They want to see participation. This isn't a tryout for the NBA or NFL! This is a chance to get beyond the realm of your TV room, or bedroom, and just get your arms and legs moving.

One time I spent an afternoon playing volleyball with some other patients. I turned a keen eye to this opportunity, essentially looking to play vigorously for a while, and then take a break. Other folks were more interested in messing around, not taking things seriously at all, and just not even staying organized. This is a key thing: staying organized, staying focused. The main reason anyone ends up in the hospital is because they can't behave properly, and behaving properly always includes an organizational component. What the attendants want to see is that you can stay within the confines of the game, keep things under control, and not get too upset if things don't go your way.

During one of my first stays, when I was sixteen, we got the opportunity to play soccer. Once again, I played a little, not getting too rambunctious. But some of the other kids decided that the best thing to do was to aim their kicks at other people. So, I just stopped playing and watched as they were reprimanded for their actions. What did this do? Well, they probably enjoyed an extra four or five days at the hospital. That's all acting out gets you - more time! Just like jail, the better you behave, the sooner you get out!

Enjoy the playtime, and don't let it get out of control. Keep a cool head even if the folks around you aren't.

Visitor Time

Visiting time was always my favorite time of the day. In the two hospitals where I was a patient, visiting time was an hour a day, every day. It's a great opportunity to see friends you haven't seen for a while, or for your parents to bring you goodies. One time my mom bought a multiple course meal from my favorite restaurant and brought enough to share with several other patients as well.

The best thing I can tell you about visiting time is that you should cherish it. It is a full hour, but that hour goes by really fast. Before you notice it, the time has passed and it is back to the same old routine. So take advantage of the time as best you can.

One time I had three sets of people I had to fit into one visiting session. So, each pair of friends got twenty minutes. This may sound kind of silly to you, but all those in question really enjoyed the time. If you haven't seen your best friends for several days, you'll find yourself cherishing the time you have.

Another time I had my best friends bring by a deck of cards and we just spent the whole hour playing Rook, a variation of Spades. We really enjoyed it, and my friends truly appreciated the opportunity to help me out. You'll find that even though you have a small amount of time to work with, everybody involved really won't mind. When you're truly sick, friends and family go out of their way to help you.

Just keep visiting time in its proper perspective. It is a chance to show everybody that you'll be back on your feet again, so try not to make mistakes. Take it from a guy who has been there: you don't want to be dragged off to the Quiet Room while your parents are standing there watching. While theoretically your parents will always love you, it is not the most respectable position to find yourself in.

Making Friends

During my first trip to the hospital at age sixteen I really didn't know how to deal with the other patients. Some of them were so off the wall that I was almost too scared to even approach them. Over time I realized that they were just kids getting the help they needed, but that first visit was a real shock to my system.

I did eventually realize that the best way to get through a stay was with a few good friends. If I was only going to be in for a short time, I would try to get close to two or three folks. Typically they would be people I had things in common with, some times not. Probably the best friend I ever made while I was in the hospital was a guy named Michael who was in for the first time. He caught me during my third trip, so by then I knew the ropes, so to speak. He was a kind, intelligent guy who was really confused about everything. He was a little older than me, and was thankful that I was there with a few choice words of advice for his stressful stay. For the last ten years Mike has called me every Christmas to chat. How did I manage to make such a good friend? I'll tell you.

I reached out. When he was crying in a corner, I would go over and give him a hug. When he asked if things would ever get better, I told him the truth – yes, but with some work. When he wondered about the deeper aspects of life (as many of us do when we're in the hospital), I would share with him my thoughts on philosophy and the meaning of everything. Mike was looking for answers, and I must have given him some that made sense, because each year my wife is blown away when he calls, yet again. And I look forward to it. I really do, because it means that I changed someone's life for the better. Nothing is more rewarding than that.

Reach out to people. Help as many folks as you can. Be the light in a dreary place. Most of the folks around you will be thankful that someone is willing to listen to what they have to say.

Your Meds

Two words: Take them!

Yes, there will be people in the hospital that will put lots of effort into not taking their meds. There will be people that lie about it, that hide them, that even try to take five out of six of their meds, all in the hopes that somehow they are accomplishing something by rebelling. Not true! Nothing is accomplished! If you try something like this, all that you are doing is slowing your progress. All that you are doing is making sure you leave later rather than sooner. One of the key things that the doctors look for is a patient that is willing to take his/her meds.

I experienced quite an adventure with my first set of meds. I slept so much that you'd think I was being paid to do it. But I didn't have any choice, because the meds took that much out of me. This situation wasn't just a week-long event, this was a four year marathon. From the age of sixteen to twenty, I spent very little time progressing with life and instead did my best not to go crazy. While in high school I had been a stellar overachiever. After I got sick I was reduced to going through college at a snail's pace, and I spent most of my time having fun. Why? I had to. If I didn't I was risking a relapse, and that would have been worse than anything. So I stuck with the meds, and eventually an amazing thing happened.

My original psychiatrist retired, and his replacement had a different opinion about what I should be taking. He put me on a new combination of meds and I could tell the difference almost immediately. During my previous four years I had put on over a hundred pounds. Within a year of having the new meds I lost that weight. My energy skyrocketed, and I was pretty close to being the old me. My college performance improved, I landed some great jobs, and life was pretty kosher. But you need to read between the lines – for four years I put up with hell. It was necessary. It had to be done. This may be necessary for you, too. If this is the case I suggest you do your best to enjoy it, because when you come out on the other side, life really does improve.

Take your meds, listen to your doctor, do what needs to be done. You'll get through it! This is a temporary situation and life really can come full circle!

Getting Discharged

Cooperate. Cooperate. COOPERATE. COOPERATE!!!!

Just do what you are told. Take it easy. Treat the hospital like a vacation, but at the same time make the changes that they suggest. In therapy and during doctor's visits you'll be asked to do some things differently. Take these suggestions to heart because they can help! The reason you are there is to get some help, so don't waste your time.

While I was in the hospital there were a few things I learned pretty quickly. They really just wanted to get two things from me: a promise not to hurt anybody, and a willingness to take medication. This is probably one of the first places you will start, too. These are the two biggies. If you can master them then you are at least guaranteed to stay alive, which is a great first step to take. Some patients never get this far, so make sure you are not one of them. Once you get these two down, you are probably just a week or so from getting out.

As I said earlier you must also learn to speak honestly with your doctor. The fastest track home is by telling your psychiatrist what is truly on your mind. If he really knows what you're thinking then he will be better equipped to prescribe the proper medications. This is key! Be up front with him, be honest, and you will be walking out the door sooner because you will be properly medicated.

Go to all the meetings, be on time for the various activities, and treat the other patients well. If you cover all of those bases, as well as the previous tips, you'll have no problem executing your exit strategy.

Getting out is a piece of cake. As you are leaving remember to thank the folks that helped you out the most. They will appreciate it!

The End

So now you've read everything I have to say. You know how to stay out of trouble, communicate with your doctors, treat other patients the way they should be treated, and use your hospital time in the most productive way possible. Everything I've conveyed in this booklet comes from my personal experience. Use these tools as I did and I hope they help you as much as they did me.

Remember, a mental hospital is not a bad place to be. You get to sleep as much as you want, eat pretty well, and make friends you wouldn't otherwise have made. As in every part of life, you are just being asked to do your job. Stick to the straight and narrow, thank those who helped you, and continue taking your prescribed meds after you leave.

The world can use more people that have beaten this illness. We need role models that are willing to stand up and declare that bipolar disorder is a beatable disease. For too many years it has gotten a bad rap for killing people, destroying families and relationships, and knocking folks out of the game of life. Be a winner! Be somebody that other folks can look up to!

During my life I've read a lot of quotes, but in my opinion only one perfectly sizes up the formula for achieving success in life:

"Never, never, never give up!" - Winston Churchill.

Appendix:
Topics To Remember

Dead Man Walking Syndrome
- where the group ostracizes the individual for whatever reason, causing uncomfortable feelings in the individual

Never Say Die Attitude
- what a bipolar patient must absolutely have to live and succeed

Medication
- complete and total acceptance that medication is now a part of life

Fun Must Be Scheduled
- having fun must now be focused on and scheduled into every day

Work Schedule
- first shift, no late night or graveyard work

Acceptance That Life Is Forever Different
- things have changed forever, adjust and move forward

Believe In The Power To Do Anything
- without it, you'll never accomplish your dreams, much less avoid the hospital

Become A Non-Violent Person
- it's too easy to lose control, so you must turn into Ghandi

Sleep As Much As You Need To
- everything else doesn't matter, sleep 14 hours if necessary

The Street Is A Reality
- it's easy to become homeless, realize that it's a reality so you can work to avoid it

Share Constantly
- let the world in on your thoughts, it will improve your life

Trust Your Doctor
- he's there to help, treat him like a friend

Use Your Day Wisely

- move forward with each day, don't waste time

No Drugs

- no drugs or alcohol, it's the only way to win

Monitor Your Thoughts

- you're the gatekeeper of your actions, it all starts with your thoughts

Set Out To Change The World

- it's easy to change yourself when your focus is on helping others

Become A Power Producer

- produce, produce, produce…it's easier to be healthy when you're working

Destroy Obstacles To Your Own Success

- become a habitual troubleshooter, it will help keep you alive

Accept and Enjoy Relationships

- life is easier with friends and family, don't push people away

Become a Competitor

- make beating bipolar disorder a personal point of pride

About The Author

Shay Villere was born in New Orleans, Louisiana. At the age of 11, his family moved to Sacramento, California. He experienced a normal childhood performing well in academics, sports, and acting. He also enjoyed having many friends.

At the age of 16, Shay was diagnosed with bipolar disorder. It occurred during his junior year of high school and eventually proved to be so severe he was forced to leave school and eventually take the California High School Proficiency Exam. Between the ages of 16 and 22 Shay was hospitalized five times for psychotic episodes. While sometimes being hospitalized for depression and mania Shay never attempted suicide.

Over the years Shay's doctors have prescribed several medications to treat his illness. At various times he has taken Lithium, Haldol, Paxil, Tegretol and Stelazine. Due to some of these prescriptions his weight has fluctuated between 180 and 310 lbs. Shay estimates it took four years to find the right combination of medications. He is now 31 years old and has carried 230 lbs. on a 6' 7" frame for the last ten years.

Shay considers himself to be a successful bipolar disorder patient. While dealing with his illness he has still managed to complete a four-year college degree program in the computer field, hold well-paying, fulfilling jobs, buy a home, marry a wonderful woman, and enjoy a beautiful young daughter! He has continued to enjoy an extended network of friends and cites his parents as the most important aspect of his support system. He has also created a Christian website dedicated to helping others: www.TheIntercessors.com.

Additional copies and contact information can be found at

www.LuLu.com/BipolarDisorder